Sons and Pioneers

IAIN BAMFORTH

Sons and Pioneers

CARCANET

First published in Great Britain in 1992 by
Carcanet Press Limited
208–212 Corn Exchange Buildings
Manchester M4 3BQ

Copyright © Iain Bamforth 1992

The right of Iain Bamforth to be identified as the author of this work has been asserted by him in accordance with the Copyright, Designs and Patents Act of 1988.

A CIP catalogue record for this book is available from the British Library.

ISBN 0 85635 995 5

The publisher acknowledges financial assistance from the Arts Council of Great Britain.

Set in Monotype Bodoni Book by Combined Arts, Edinburgh.

Printed and bound in England by SRP Ltd, Exeter.

to Barbara and Christian Schütze

Er fürchtet, er werde zwar als Abraham mit dem Sohne ausreiten,
aber auf dem Weg sich in Don Quichotte verwandeln.

Kafka

Acknowledgements and Notes

Thanks are due to the editors of the following publications in which some of these poems, or earlier versions, first appeared: *The Age* (Melbourne), *Cencrastus*, *Honest Ulsterman*, *Oxford Magazine*, *PN Review*, *Poetry Review*, *Quadrant* (Sydney), *Times Literary Supplement* and *Verse*.

'No Man's Wise' is a recombinant version of the Anglo-Saxon poem *The Wanderer*; lines 64–65 supplied the title and last line, in contracted form, as well as encoding the rest of the poem. The title 'Bags and Iron' is a locution occurring in Patrick White's memoir *The Prodigal Son*. The Brecht poem 'Der Zweifler' can be found on p. 587 of the Suhrkamp volume *Gedichte in einem Band*. Gottfried Benn's poem 'Ein Land –' appears on p. 241 of the Fischer Verlag imprint, *Gedichte in der Fassung der Erstdrucke*. For the shamanistic scat-song formulas in 'Snake' and 'Bring your Horse', and for other source material, I am indebted to *Shaking the Pumpkin*, Jerome Rothenburg's anthology of Amerindian poetry.

Contents

I

Men on Fire

Being a land of dissent and magnificent defeats
it evolved a subtle theology of failure, stealing its own thunder
wherever two or three were gathered together
and the occult plumbing groaned querulously beneath the boards.

These days, it grows owlish with hindsight –
recounting itself as a salvo of rain far north on mappamundi,
who's who of a supernumerary Creation myth
that swallowed the serpent's tail, ate the offspring whole.

When Rousseau exhumed the weather over Waverley
its civil imaginary became a fast diminishing return.
Few Encyclopaedists recall the genealogy backpacked out of Troy
or the vernacular of a silver-tongued Golden Age.

Later it saw itself arsy-versy, a nation after the letter;
but common cause outreaching the Dutch
it sold its birthright for a cut of the glory...
a mere idea, it seemed invincible.

Yet it thrived on its own lost cause, and the mark of Cain
was a lefthandedness it practised righteously –
its sentinel cities on the plain a gritty paradigm
for an industry of calloused hands.

Guilt was one thing it exported to the new world;
ballast to the quantum energy ascending through midnight suns
as a monument of candour, men on fire:
here, in the old, sorrow recurs as a brief downpour,

dream-fug, supplements to a Journal of the Plague Year
when the gospel of virtues, that manic uprightness,
laid blame at nobody's door but its own...
beyond reach of heaven was a legislature pining for hell.

Out of it, sons and daughters have no clear sighting
of how an apple-tree opens the debate
but know it does, since they find themselves
on a mission without a motor, reciting the plot backwards

while pavements become rain-sleeked and lustral
and an oddly buoyant cargo gospel
swims through anti-matter to the hard edge of the landscape.
Like a native technology, it starts from what's left

and salvages its own future, a startled Doric narrative
stalking the wet track, tongue and tinder
to its radical children, shy to touch the incontrovertible ores
of a faith that has lately outgrown its disappointment.

Life in a Box

'regret and corpuscles'
  – Celine

1.
Ill, but never ill
enough, said one

they begged for health
but believed in sickness

pink puffers, blue bloaters
we'd teach them how

to pass through pain
and be responsible, said another

principle's black stranglehold
on the solar plexus

2.
Choirs of flowers
were chanting for the rest

they might get better
but they'd never get well:

at night some tried
to slip away, wrapped in flags

of surrender: before
the state reclaimed them

they lay in our museum
dry with desire

3.
Lives gone septic, lives
left out in the rain –

given half a chance they'd
blurt it out, how

they'd botched the one
that might have been theirs

or someone else's –
coughing and very far away

the slamming of doors
and people punishing their bodies

4.
No body; no story –
nothing could be done

till we had the facts:
what we offered was famously

a matter of interpretation
(a Latin doggerel

hexed by the eye of Horus)
holding them on beds

and probing the hurt
that seemed to fit the life

5.
Compassion's scutwork
and the rhetoric of pathos

death was a late afternoon
of morphine and flies

Go deep, said our critics
sport the taut look

of accomplices: one day
suffering would be a secret

everybody understood –
same gaffe, twice over

6.
Life: it was in a box
we let it take a breather

from the oppression of white
and the Book of Diseases

where the subtle teleological
warmth of cold steel

was a pastoral theme –
pre-emptive, cautionary,

like the anger of a revolution
in a high-ceilinged room

The Runners

Get up, go out into the dark
beneath the domed asylum of the sky
not quite remembering, not understanding why.

You'll have to write it on the hoof,
the life you leave behind. Now you shout
it isn't mine; but it is, it is —

the profile of the day slack-jawed
with disbelief, the finebone crockery
on tenterhooks. Don't hesitate and ponder

what the old hurt means. It means
you have to go and pull the mountains down,
leave hamlets haunted by your teatime

parricide. Walk down the drive
past clumps of rhododendrons shivering
like idiot sentinels. Lock the gate

on childhood's apparatus of admittance,
grey hours when milkmen come
and the fridge whines quietly to itself.

The big house is empty. Crestfallen
gables say it, and the knocking pipes:
years go to pot, or learn to read

the landscape crow-legged on your face.
They stalk the morning on an old clay road,
each hill resounding with the perfect

unanimity of silence. Now it comes clear,
denounced by names in the graveyard
and the yelps of village dogs —

there's no victory, though under tarpaulin
manoeuvres still go on, someone might recover
the elusive third meaning and tomorrow

gobbing its small discrepancies of light
on all believers. Not quite, ever.
The runners aren't coming, the stars lied –

you'll have to festinate to another
place. What's there is this: the absurd sea
shuffling like a palsy over cattle-tracks,

pollen shaken out by the tundra's rim,
sweetnesses of juniper and a wrecked car
teetering on a final bluff. Nobody

preaches there who isn't strong enough to
die, squirming on his makeshift cross
or sailing away with the washing.

Dungheaps steam with mystifications;
garrulous rivers leap out of culverts
to bleat a reprimand. Recall the promises

you failed to keep. Feel them on your face
in the ravines of the Great Killing
or by the Atlantic, heaving around Cape

Wrath. The dead are guesting at the watertables
of the moles. Miles overhead a cloud insists
that you must go, that you must stay

and punish the pillows. What's done comes
too: all down the day, down all the days
till that hedged no becomes a way

of saying yes. New year brings up the old;
the sun commemorates on terminal moraines
each flinty verdict. You shake the air

and watch the trees shed last night's rain.
So: no return, but the place you find
will be the place you left behind.

Sí Señor

They tear the ban from the notary
with a grand gesture to impress their mothers
standing below the much-kissed Virgin
and the cross slowly sinking into the facade
of the only arcade in town –
where the Avenue of the Morning of the Republic
spreadeagles the Way of All Sinners.
Unruffled, sisters sweat in the ice-room.
Others clustered at the drugstore
offer nothing but themselves.
Moths cling to their off-white linen frocks
and to the newspaper abandoned
by the franchise holder now lighting a cheroot
in front of the waxwork museum.
As evening falls on the rest of the day
they unnail the Son of Man
and drag His wooden body through the streets
where leaves will whisper scandal
and rain seems news of somewhere else
in the house with electricity.
After a hundred years of dying exotically
instead of roads, fields, horizons,
they might be discussing capital and combines
and the permutations of the lottery.
With the Judas kiss, when the truth spills out,
old women huddle anxiously around
for the moon's benediction, the Bible-talk
of fever winds and slapped fish
and the Saviour walking across swamps;
but when an entire town empties into the square –
literal, vituperous, unanimous –
beneath a pageant of parasols and hombergs,
it's poised, like a man stepping into a woman,
for the assassination of reality.

Brothers and Sisters

That this walked down the mountain
of our common guilt-culture
with its quick dispraise and cold
evacuations of the spirit
would have surprised even them.

No, it wasn't a children's crusade
or New England pastoral
though it wept something of stalled
destiny, the millenarianism
that avoids captives or converts...

Men moved when God moved each,
dressed, hitched the wagons and went
teetering into the near-distance,
mahogany trestles upended
like creaking heifer carcasses.

Brothers consorted with sisters –
how to break Isaac's back
without cajolement, without disdain.
Heirlooms juddered on the shelves
and windows bent with light.

They slept together like spoons,
wondering hugely at the wet
books of cities, trams and steam
and the corporation gasworks
sighing into the twentieth century.

Beyond the reach of their knowing
they became themselves, new men
on old earth, hope about to happen –
falling out of mind, and history,
and the past they never had.

Jesus Wept

A painstaking people of cramped means,
ruminant memory, curt miscomprehensions:

shamefaced inquisitors of the word-shy
who stood by the dead, God's promissory.

★

Teetotalers, desperados, glum glee-men,
tongue-tied mummers who held their own.

They conjured names, hoarded one-liners.
Eloquence split raw against the grain.

★

Death duties amassed for the afterlife.
In that guild of stutterers, no-hopers,

I longed for the hot effluent of tears,
the slow sleepwalk of heavenly trespass.

★

Caulked liberty tree of the waterlogged,
thousands who begged to ride the whale.

They shrank from the light like Lazarus
or eavesdropped while the summer chafed.

★

Weekends, they covenanted to God's house
and found its proof had gone to ground.

They gave me a cold shoulder to lean on;
a vagrant climate that had come indoors.

★

Gravity's spill. Rehearsals, keepsakes;
petrified script of the once-startled.

I sneaked back to peek at the dumb-show,
hand-me-down alibis for a kingdom come.

★

Soul-salvagers, grim Sabbath gazeteers.
They stood me up to knock me down again

until I understood the justifying pain,
its rectitude, its dust-dry settlements.

★

I said my small Amen, and seized the day,
and bit my tongue so hard it shouted out

how Jesus wept among the boiling fields
– chorus and citizen, righter of wrongs.

The Great Exhibition

It was their Zion, the dream-life of capital.
As I watched, it hurtled out of the steam age
and nudged the latitudinarians botanizing on the asphalt

(Faith, Hope and Charity, my three Chekhovian sisters:
the bulk of the new century left them asthmatic
as if they'd spent the morning underground).

Aviators sprouted wind-buds, like the dodo,
and an archaeologist threading back from the hippocampus
found Calcutta's revenue sinking into the Jurassic.

Best to be an engineer, standing a street on end.
At the Great Exhibition a crowd went hoarse
in front of a shiny automat for operating old ethics.

My father took me there, monopolized the zinc;
I squinted uneasily into my own grave
or floated on hot air above a row of upturned faces.

I could hear nothing but handshakes being shed
and the parrot-screech of my dowager aunt
living off the capital, in a Zulu dream.

Mother was propped on the pillows with Mr Micawber;
her whalebones heaving with the love-death
while the day congealed like butcher's dripping.

It seemed a congress of spiritualists;
sublime small talk teetering on the ridiculous –
Money and Meaning, shareholders of the new Jerusalem

where Nature was disrobed for Science
and a century submitted to its absentee landlord
that if kept marching, it would rise to heaven.

Thunder and Lightning

The hope of it held him,
frowning at the door, setting out

like good brother Bunyan
to tumble the hills about with words.

What was soldered to the landscape were
names: strangers', pilgrims'.

He sat on the fence, trespassing.
He couldn't tell the names

though the fields knew them all, casting
no intelligible shadows. Wind came

and seditious birds, and furnished them.
In the pit it was still starry.

He leant on the plough and heard the sea,
its suck and spend. A head

was in his hands, and the head said his.
The day was superb and the sun.

He noised abroad. Wind came
and sober rain, and cooled his head.

One day he'd peddle thunder.
Wife and children waited by the door.

The Doubter

(Bertolt Brecht)

Whenever we seemed
To have hit on the answer to a question
One of us loosened the binding of the matted old
Chinese wall-hanging: it would unfurl
And we all saw the man on the bench who
Doubted so completely.

What he told us was this:
I'm the Doubter. I'm in two minds whether
You ever scribbled *Finis* on the work that almost finished you.
Whether what you said put any other way would still carry weight.
Whether you said it well but nevertheless
Thought the truth of what you said a bit slippery?
Whether it isn't ambiguous; for every potential misunderstanding
You'll take the rap. But then, if it's unambiguous
It may smooth the snags out of things: is it too unambiguous?
If it is, then what you say is useless. It's a non-starter.
Are you really in the swim of what's happening? On terms with
What's in the making? Are you changing? Who are you anyway? Whom
Are you addressing? Who can use what you're saying? And
    furthermore:
Is it sober-headed? Can it be read in the morning?
Does it take up from what's already there? Are the lines
You're hearing made use of, or at least refuted? Can everything be
    verified?
By experience? Which one then? But above all
Always above all else: what do they do
If they believe what you say? Above all: what do they do?

Mulling it over, curious, we studied the doubting
Blue man on the wall-hanging, gazed at each other and
Started again from scratch.

Calvinist Geography

– A northern supremacist monad!
It eavesdrops, shrewd dissertation:
goes out to shoot converts
when light drips through the roof
and the day leans to, a gob
of consternation at the easy drama

of the dark. Novel as any nation
it grows on you like a fuggy absence,
archaic body, story's end.
What's left limps back to first
causes, the old betrayals –
though no one's wiser now

the fire's smoored and a soft smirr
drifts in across the moors. *Or
it blows wrong, a chill family epic
kept wrapped for redemption:
when the renegade sermons start up
again, from clumps of rock*

*and scraggy deserts between estates,
they tell you more than you want
to know about persistence
and extinction, the risen towns
gravid with herring, crazed fiddlers
making a palaver in the square –*

*or here on one of Wade's roads
where the servile myths skite home
to sour news, the barracking
of a threadbare ruinous country.*
It holds an accent out, in self-defence.
Sweet as failure, you can taste

feral voices on the tongue:
success, they say, will always
ring a hollow change, like sorrow.
Attrition, diaspora: they're children
from an illfitting marriage;
shipped off to weather continents

without a say-so in the sublimations
of unreadiness. Trite tradition,
it leaves its interpreters
stuck on voes, shouting across islands
for the pure light of justice.
Underfoot, it's the usual unison,

granite voices thinking they're already
home, though the sun could tell
why happiness is hostile. Hard
breathing, flight's nervous feathers,
always get goosed. *Wind scolds*
like a mother, and soon the moon

has pale ideas of its own, none new
to the narrator. Names are maps
among the oxbows and civic drumlins;
open secrets. They inhale
suprise, subtilized by circumstance,
a blunt determination to make good

that could easily spend another century
riddling for old catastrophes,
cleared spaces, idylls, odd ideals.
There's no new peak, hardly even
a pent Sunday or an underground edition.
Irony's a glib surface like the sea:

a spit of land, a cold promontory
where goodness has to be spat on too
when the day's done. *No thought
of comfort or compensation:
the joke about deserters wasn't one.*
Work it out, then: either rescue it

from its talk of beginnings or know
you might be right, being wrong.
*It drives off through rain
and conflagrations, in all directions,
passes proof to the snug compass.*
Now it's dark it's almost dawn.

II

Legal Tender

1.

My mother, a dark-haired pamphleteer
with a Book of Numbers name
crammed in Adam Smith and Marx

on the radical short-straw of capital
before she went home to God the Father
and the rain-king thunderings

on the floorboards. Small wonder
I always thought of her later in life
curled up for a bushel at the feet of Boaz,

my Anglo-Saxon father, a deserter
from the New Model Army. Victory would be
his, outfacing the motherland.

2.

Why the thirteenth tribe had decamped
to one of Antonine's hill-forts
was, as someone said, another question.

Aunts and uncles, brothers and sisters,
we were all prone to exaggeration.
Having breached silence to put a foot

in the twentieth century, there was no
way back to the starry-eyed families
at Shiloh. After the pitch dark

and cold chill, the time would come
when we'd walk out on the world
like a parable of our own understanding.

3.
We thought the faith was granite;
it was soft sandstone, pocked by rain
and buffeted by insults. We read our lunatic

expropriations from the annals of desire,
Great Bedlam's almanac of bygones.
Sorrow was consequential. Taxed with God's

own equities, we were as quick to fault
as to forgive – though only ourselves –
getting up bleary-eyed at 6 o'clock

to meet the man in Shields Road.
Not that he ever kept an appointment,
half-deaf, who'd never read his Romans.

4.
Our house glared at the Sleeping Warrior,
the highlands shivering in the rain.
The Clerk of Session had left his name

on the entire district, playing off
a bold republic of unlikelihood
with the about-face of a nearly-nation.

False prophet! He'd slipped the censors
somewhere between the infinitely slow
smoulder of Foxe's *Book of Martyrs*

and Bunyan in his damp prison fastness:
no metaphor surviving stone drill
except the one about the living rock.

5.
As a small boy I had one trick
when they couldn't manufacture my consent.
It stonewalled their off-political

recipes of awe, back-biting grievances
of a country too small to afford
the myth of its own largesse. Silence,

and then the waiting curdled faces
of the chosen few. Even the Atlantic
mislaid itself, whispering Clydewide.

And I would think of stealing downstairs
to find them all gone, silence
having stacked the dishes in the sink.

6.
Pending the limelight of the final audit
we comforted each other with bright
sagas of ultimate compensation.

Despair was the one sin we didn't dare
and we hardly wondered how it was,
living in the world. On the wall the deeds

were a slapstick funeral ban, triumphal
chitchat in a disjunct Mesopotamian
dialect. Only a desperado would pretend

to be elsewhere, scouring his tongue.
Legal tender was my mother kneading out
one justice for the literalminded.

7.
God was history's caesura, a breathtaking
ambush. I longed to be a heckler
shouting out the gainsay of infant

convictions, glacial elements.
It wasn't theatre when they stopped short
waiting for history to hurl them

into rapture. But it was, and feet
got washed. I feared the lookout vigilance
of the son who'd soared beyond hypothesis.

He dragged us down by the roots,
our fallacies of spontaneous generation –
elective, selective nostalgias.

8.
I was always blowing my own trumpet.
Nothing could set me free again like faith
or seize my share of the rain-blanket

when I threw a pomegranate in their laps
and stalked out – a shy upstart
groping for courage, rain on my face,

as if one day at the world's end
with the sun steaming into the Atlantic
and the moon smashed on the tiles

I'd come crowding back to a locked door
and an empty mothballed bedroom
in my makeless country, wide of the Word.

Mandate for Mending

As is, it isn't, couldn't be. Small wonder
it gets mislaid, if never quite as lost
as the draft-original, invented for export

but waiting, waiting, slant as truth
or mum taking in the washing on a Sunday;
it's waiting for reinstatement. What it reads

is what it reads against: human bondage,
kindnesses that kill, and giving up the ghost.
It rustles in and raids your head –

a mischief, a minority, never more alert
when in dudgeon, spelling postponement
and a curse on all houses. Moral

as hindsight, and the eerie sons of light,
Sabbath and sermon and the mean
of every hypothesis. Vitriol for citizens

in their penury of nations: it sells, transmuted
by barley and mould, a last rehearsal
for independence day. Words without comment

and children packed off to bed; weekends
when they'd spit it out: history for virgins.
Like a put-down in Tacitus, war surplus

and cold comfort; it rings a sardonic joke
at the neighbour's wake though hardly a foot
treads the Gaelic whale-songs. Desperate

and dark, then, its northern reason; a tune
for wailing in Canada or down-under
whenever the pauses get pregnant. It comes to

west of itself, trawling a gnarled accent
through a freakish bag of winds:
no sooner kidnapped than it reappears

in miners' diaries, among the waterlogged
everywhere. Of false starts and fresh starts
no further talk. Only the ending gets

tripped over in the large outdoors of bright
shouts, mendings, words like this
and that, meaning what they can't prevent.

The American Hospital

First defumigate the patient. Then blow softly
into his ear. Finally, lay on your hands.

That was how Tom, the shaman I'd hardly credit,
went down among the earth-spirits, bone-tired

of raising the dead. Apollo or Ascelpius,
the gods of medicine were lyric embarrassments...

What I had was a chalk placebo, dog-eared
mantras of cheerfulness and the clinical ritual

of second opinions. Style and fascination;
no, they were literary curses: as a punishment

fame screened me over and over again
the life-story called failure. The other story

was an indiscretion among the pale chlorine
shades of the hospital where half of Europe's

rich went subterfuge. Puritan in white,
I'd be their guide, and the oneness of function

my only text. Promise held its breath
when fear set out on its hot-foot journeys

to the airy bedrooms. Bodies emptied, slipping
into the furniture. I held their breath

when they went, caught myself in the simple
facts of loss. Another licensed voyeur.

A Plain Man's Guide to the Millennium
for Douglas Shenson

Vikings are doomed in deeper latitudes
but starlings can still be tracked to a window-ledge
in a city moored like the Marie Celeste
on edgy America, an economy that upends gravity
for a cartesian view of the vortex;
under celluloid, a pure conjectural haze.

Out of the coughing rooms on Ellis Island
soars a manic whisper of the ideal mind.
Gawk-eyed tourists congregate on a granite bed
as the electorate dismisses its refugee councillors
to watch another airy masterpiece
on the six basic rules of Esperanto grammar.

Recently it has all hardened into permanent lateness,
crying back to the stern-faced fathers;
on shabby wharves the homeless pay amends
beneath a full-moon's vertigo,
unaware of Moses' uptown grandiose nightmares
or the way out to the vivarium suburbs.

Every leap-year someone reads back to Trotsky on 164th,
Freud's mistake, and the reconstructed Oklahoma Nature Theater.
Aabrahamson and Zyziak point out the tollbooth
to a guided tour of how the West was won;
go in and you'll come out again
thinking tomorrow must have been a postal address.

A glacier slowly shifts down Broadway's canyon floor.
Neon Cupids shoot you through the heart
and mile-long convoys in irritable immobile rows
hint to heaven with their horns
that Business must always go on as usual.
Petrified capital towers above your draughty head.

Quoting themselves, buildings guy an era's helium,
monuments to the rapture still springing up between lots.
Glass and mock-renaissance brickwork
hide behind all kinds of extravagant plumbing,
places where the spirit astounds itself
living on the outside, impermeable as the future.

Yet there are vaults that have never been unsealed.
Buckling though the asphalt crust
archives recapitulate a century's civic endeavour.
Outside, their neoclassical stucco
tries to confuse the immense tonnage of anxiety
with a hyperventilating access of summer.

Ignoring red and greeen quotation marks
Jefferson's children find their eyes lured upwards.
All that's lacking is a mountain within hailing distance,
a giant upstaged by King-Kong antics on the roof
where nothing's vandalized and the vista
floats on a sea of soporific noise.

On the Hudson, armadas are putting out to sea
though they won't find it easier there
to update the survival manuals;
some hoist the trademark, others toast Bartholdi's mother.
Onshore breezes heap throwaways at their feet
while fathoms below, a city's conscience silts the Atlantic.

Rentable silences are never absolute
but New York's sheer hyperbole reaches up to scrape the clouds.
When the grid goes down, families emerge from the ziggurats
on the outlandish edge of its hanging gardens
and dreams play back in real time
among their furniture squatting in the street.

Tabloids have written off the late lamented Brecht
and declared that one man's misery is another's lucky break:
on a rickety soapbox in the park

a preacher still hawks the love that laid down its life,
though someone is starting to shout him down.
He digs deeper into bottomless pockets of kindness.

He calls their bluff, to hover above a manhole
while he winds the story back to Adam's navel
and the word-bazaars of Babel.
He asks them what they'll say when they meet the man
and the dead come crowding back
to haunt their triumphant statistical brio.

No one stands aloof, least of all the semiologists of bliss
biting into the citrus zest of lost allure.
Potholing through Le Corbusier's Radiant City
they stumble across a labyrinth for absentminded minotaurs,
a ghostly waft of tribal pass-words
and the sad comic lisp of the past's double-Dutch.

Faces that were rigid sag under rainy glissandi.
Happiness is duty-bound, a right of way –
nobody bats an eye at the weatherman's heresies
or how he monopolizes the hopeful barometric contours
of that broad denominator, the horizontal time
that hasn't been walked in decades now.

Beyond it they're rehearsing a crowd-scene for a movie
on the unending pursuit of copyright:
between decibel readings, look up again
at yesterday getting wrecked
so you can dream it back to your one horse town
where differences too, are a thing of the past.

Walk out, then, thinking you're a free man,
into the gob-smacking gossip of rising expectations.
Only meliorists erase their own graffiti.
Lorca's peering down a fire-escape
at the roller-coaster called the twentieth century;
where he walked out, he fell into the sky.

Though nobody shouts it out, there's no escape
from purple talk when the credits roll:
thunderous canticles of air rise along ice-floes
where misfortune's a windchill
haunting Seneca in the hunting grounds;
elsewhere it moans for a life beyond television.

Not a spoor remains of Minnewit's stockades
or the yellow taxis that drove the huddled hordes indoors.
Self-help's an axiom of helplessness:
in the ghost trains to the fourth world
bag people trade options, extras without a permit
for the cold comfort of strangers.

A city strains westwards, to the end of its tether.
Its sponsors read between the lines and croon the blues
of mornings-after and the Four Last Things.
At the end of the line another pioneer slips away
without a thought for the future
or the untidy past breaking loose again with a hallelujah.

Everything is achieved, out in the open.
Mickey-mockers and problem-solvers have heard it before,
the story of how it is: one long awkward silence
when the penny-plain looks across the language
soon to step ashore
in a make-believe of true believers.

In the House of the Sun

A fossil sea went up in smoke
but we got there in the end, sick

of stucco and stale Havanas.
We had come that year to adore the sun.

The mayor was a wino whose spit
was sour mesquite, hand on his gun

to extol the one-way traffic of the sun,
its pure expenditure. It seemed

we'd arrived before the railroad
but the sun went about its business anyway,

crisping the faces of the mestizos
who'd colonized the forest floor.

The next day, and for years after,
we followed the swarms of blowflies

buttoning a furious charivari
on the natives, raw in the undergrowth.

They weren't sleeping, just lipreading
the equinox that hacked away their hearts,

the glut-god of all economies
leering down from the topmost branches.

What we owed, they'd had to pay...
Solar, we idled northwards in a jeep

where the petrifactions of old America
bristled with names we'd lifted:

Quetzalcóatl and Xolotl and a sea
of maize moaning in the wind,

women with tattoos anticipating
a mouth to mouth manoeuvre in the dark.

A Parable of Street Wisdom

What is anger for? I asked the wise man
    walking on the mountains.
He frowned at me and pointed to the stones.
    Far away I counted boats
dwindling like hypotheses on the open sea,
    and beside me the wise man,
head on his stone, recanting the old religion.
    Still I didn't know anger.

What is anger for? I asked the several people
    standing in the street.
The people was a thicket huddled round its need.
    Dull wet came down, and dark,
and one by one, the thousand trod its thoughts
    from kind to harm to blame.
Then my feet told me: even puddles resent the sky
    and the acquiescing clouds.

So I went into the desert, where the one sun
    dictates to conscience,
and asked God. The sea was standing on its head.
    He answered with a question.
Does the rain have a father? In the hot quiet
    I lifted up my voice and wept,
and the sea came in, softly closing the door
    to tell me my punishment.

Days

Like Uz and Buz most tread the furlong between the Tree of Knowledge and the Tree of Life; one upholding the vow, the other teasing out a riddle.

A few, like the Ugliest Man, always take another furrow: revenge on the witness. Meaning runs to catch them up and never does. As in the Book, they die, old and full of themselves.

Shoulder to the wheel, their Sanskrit version has been peddled round a quern without anyone ever coveting its barrows of rain.

Imagine a wisdom too shamefaced to bring back home.

They will leave us to ourselves soon enough, bruising the door or bundling up the air like Shem's daughters, yeasty with reproaches.

With only themselves to outreach nobody dares introduce them to their own deception.

Evening falls to its death in a crevice; a thought comes to nothing. But that's not how it is. Ask Uz or Buz.

Like chalk horses, they get led over the hill, beyond the offence and the expiatory tidbits. Bare hands walk across them.

At night, they're dense giants, working through silence. They leave no bones though they bruise, still believing in the enemy.

Signing truce is an old imposture of eagles and jaguars.

(Only Abraham would understand: perfect obedience is always a temptation).

Going, they arrange their transport – beds on their backs like a river sagging with bridges. Here, under one, is the zigzag life-sign secreted by Long Rain to his wife, in another epic.

Wet and welter, our old curriculum. An altogether opening nakedness.

No Man's Wise
A legend

Man moves, crooked, through the cramped
seasons, down to his doom,
and the earth rolls over, not to hear the pale
shouts for help, wrecks of spars
in the brightly burning cities.
What's given there gets taken away.
He tangles heart with hurt
and sees it form in the mud like thought,
his walk, his weird.
A fire catches by the river.

Flushed things die back to a skeleton winter.
Across the hills hands dig for dark.
Wolves howl to hunters;
strangers wait at wet stations
for knack and knowing,
bile-stiff hands pointing out the way
down clarted drove-paths
to a sky no higher than the ceiling,
actual rain and disagreements,
old backward arguments.

On the seventh day he packs his things.
Goose-fleshed, the wind calls back,
a hammer hand above dull roofs
that never break curfew
but watch him go, clothing him in clouds;
no monk, on the path of righteousness,
heaving cargo on his back,
but muddled man with bone to pick
across sheer mountains, seas like sludge.
Life's proved by risking it.

In the north, dim days pile up like cairns.
What calendars promise
are paper dragons, tired to tell.
Heart isn't in it, but heart still does it:
crust on snow, against
a snell east wind, like no salt hero
or outcast son or messenger,
feet-stamping he comes, grizzled as custom
to an estuary where spirits cry
and trees make supplications to the wind.

He thinks he's home, in sleep or clouds,
where living is the look
laying no welcome, useless as said.
He draws the evening up around his head
and the hush is talk of him:
goad at the gate, rough hands to come.
Low voices hold the law. He gets up to go
but can't, since in the act,
he must renounce it, all year down.
No man's wise before winter.

Pneumatic
Halway sheyamod

All night I'd been poring over the proofs
for my *Vade Mecum of Cultural Quanta*

and under the halogen of a 40-watt bulb
swanning coolly down the Liffey

like a relative of Rudolf Virag
lately of Szombathély, Vienna, Milan, etc

and soon to be a cultivator of orange
plantations in the Negev desert.

I might just have well been orbiting
a whirly-whirly in Swahili

or reading a back-issue of *la Mondlingvisto*
(dated Sofia 1899) for the sense

I was making. My rock logic was leaky.
Why didn't Yiddish have a word

for war? Where was Urquhart on
or around the week of October 5th, 1582?

It was enough to make anyone go back to
Go. What I was sitting on were *capitaux*

fébriles: zeroes imported from cochinchina
in a sack of dried peppercorns.

That was when I stumbled across plans
to fireproof the great Golgonooza

and drafts for an *a posteriori* language
in which 'I'm yours' is a plain

1–80–17. The rest of the night I spent
describing the colour red, wooing

you back with a moon-eyed line from Rami
and an excerpt out of the Talmud

where God says, after 26 attempts,
'Let's hope it works'. (In any language

soul-talk's a primitive breath-sound,
a whoop of joy or a catarrhal *Pprrpffrrpfff*

when the big ideas go for broke.) Sleep
on it: Scheherazade's whoopy cushion

that trampolines us to the vertigo
of pure attentiveness, an aerosol exhalation

when you sneeze and a soul stands naked,
as if to say *God's a verb, not a noun.*

Foreign Bodies

Tongue in cheek
we resuscitated the old myths;
even then their meaning leaked away.

★

We cannibalized the one-off histories
of our glutinous bodies,
each in the other's language.

★

In my oral tradition
there was only one way home.
You'd already thrown away the ladder.

★

Innocence was branded
like a hoof on my forehead:
Werther's guide to the Beautiful World.

★

You walked my spine like an Aztec
for the braille of solidarity;
I sent morse signals back.

★

A trapped, explicit odour:
we sleuthed down the startled spoor
of its volatile hush-hush.

★

When you couched against my pelvis
a militant chorus of birds
swam gracefully away.

★

Outside, under the lacteal stars,
there were no alibis,
only precincts for throat-clearing.

★

You wore the names of Job's daughters:
Dove, Cinnamon, Eye-shadow.
Love was a camp-follower.

★

A steady-state where tenses changed,
an enzyme pungency
of inspissated mucus sighs.

★

The moon was in a sweat.
We gazed across the sheets
at our bodies, obvious as Egypt's.

★

It was an easy sell,
our inappropriate technology.
What it hadn't mastered was desire.

★

I stalled on your nakedness.
Eloquent, you sat among the furniture
betraying your sympathies.

★

Hunchbacked, like Zeno the Eleatic
and Monkey's zero-sum epic:
one about to swallow the other.

★

Exaltation and terror –
two tenses of a reflexive grammar
misconstrued by the translator.

★

Our pillow politics were everyone's,
lingering like Zeus
on Europa, her soft-mouthed insults.

★

There could be nothing between us.
Distance was understood
yet almost as quickly misunderstood.

★

All the time we'd been staging a hearing
for Nabokov's erotic phoneme,
a nonce in any language.

★

Joy in the 20th century –
a relic, like a Kalapuya ghost dance.
(Favourite bedtime reading.)

★

There was nothing to declare.
Even our arrival was a play on words,
baggageless but for the road.

Alone among Revivalists

Next time, come yourself; don't send your son. Yesterday's boat people
steered across the Atlantic to translate that homily
back to Canaan, though nobody had warned them: one scripture baked
in the fiery furnace of a never-nevertheless land

would devour the plains and mountains with a fierceness
that never named itself presumption, far less infamy. Even if the wind
keened with the north-south objectivity of iron
in the compass, there was no gainsaying the anti-gravities of light

and haemoglobin. So they hung the language out to dry
and at night, across the prairie, wolves bayed plainsongs on the long
immiseration of togetherness. Nothing, it seemed, could deflect
the zodiac of good intentions, the contagious humour

of disbelief – though when the neighbourhood glacier
stopped shunting their city of chrome and caustic
into neat hills of rubble, they caught a sense of what was meant
by the stony-faced law of judges and why

what should have been a promise now menaced them,
thundering its petulant retort not across the horizon, but vertically.
They'd missed their cue, and all that was left
was to caravan back to reality, to die in the wrong order

well before the coming of the host. Suburbs cropped up for miles
        around
and the climate was a black mood of longing, hats tilted
against the welfare state. Once in a while
they took a long look back and called it progress, as if hope

could be ardent after fearful baptisms, immersion in the fact.
Sunsets were an enormous red. The river would never be still
or stepped in twice. Leaving behind that era
of handbills and self-made men, they groped back to the high ground

where fear was made to fly and the outcasts left to the wolves.
Believing, they'd been seared by a blast from the furnace door. Freedom
meant this: being less than any nation. They'd got as far
as they were going to get, and their finned cars

would glide them through the cotton fields. The day was old
but the story older. Imagine, then: tomorrow's maps drawn to the
  levantine
time of the covenant, a screen of trees snaring the wind
and the ocean coldly receptive. Clouds would be their great machinery

and destiny a footnote to the hazards of the course,
tempest and doldrums and the stars surging up to hang nervously
in the right place, guiding them. They ploughed an ocean
and nobody smelled a fish. Prayed together, where the waves
  collapse.

III

Alibis

It was a barely perceptible affront.
Mr Wordly Wiseman took sentimental fright
in the arms of a carnival victim who spoke no English
and a bulemic variety of the patois...
métro, boulot, dodo of an hexagonal affair.

Beneath my window, the Street of the Dry Tree
led down to the Pont Neuf: new to the *ancien régime*
and still new to a discredited 18th Brumaire –
those bourgeois sins, complacency and self-regard,
strode out of their century, asking why we needed this...

The other side, past the eviscerated belly of Paris,
was a tour through the skin trade: fast food, fast sex
and a gallic Punch giving Judy the once-over;
little secrets Maigret might have kept from his wife
and the big-time vendors of the naked truth.

By the door, I'd stacked the empties, my cadavers.
I was reading Brecht on the hell of the disenchanters
and watching my deaf-dumb neighbour watching me...
Twice weekly to buy milk, and long afternoon surveillances
till the pigeons hauled the daylight home.

Every evening, I drowsed to an upstairs *Liebestod*.
Someone was dreaming of being a frontiersman in America
or stalking Flaubert to the lower reaches of the Nile:
watermarks on the wall of the local morgue.
Tracking sun-spots, I compounded my dream-interest.

I was glossing the storyline as fast as I dared
in a place my grandpa called Babylon, the Antichrist *chez lui*.
Deaf to domesdays, it was still crossing itself
or chafing the epochs like a cod-accordion...
scraping by on Piaf-naif dreams of glory.

To the silent majority this was never the End-of-Days.
In Figaro's marriage, their namesakes had forced the hand;
centuries later they were still living off the dowry...
That retro-radical flight from history
was the snore of the old world outliving itself.

Before the continental drift of two wars
I could imagine Nerval trailing home his livid lobster
to a draughty grammar and the past's Latin drone.
After Haussmann, every lamppost was an orator
interrogating the breezy dispersal of the Communards.

Candid, the swans hissed from the oil-slicked Seine
and made me a duvet beneath the rafters.
After the rest went south one always stayed behind,
its head beneath its wing, flim-flamming the current;
undemocratic, a hesitant Belgian joke.

Halfheartedly I studied the semiotics of couscous
or watched the French devour their colonies.
I bore my life to the Deux Magots and left the ashes there;
a diagram of detours, another unfinished novel.
I took a visceral interest in my precarious species.

Curdled leftovers occluded the windowsill.
Whatever they meant was there to keep me in my place
till the damp became a sticky resurrection.
In one myth of the private life I was killing time
till I joined them in exhaustion, passion's last logic.

Better to play the medicine man, overhauling the rich
with pop-Oedipal recipes out of Dr Pangloss.
I listened to the histories of hundreds of bodies,
anaesthetic, *involontaire*, subsumed in the mesmeric aura
of everlasting life, an odd entropic metaphor.

Back came the comic echo, news of my four bare walls...
I was a novice, fingering the sacramental relics,
eaten whole by the culture fetishists.
Satisfaction was the gape-mouthed, cruel, pacific god
who gave me everything, even the need itself.

And art or absinthe a way of swamping Giant Despair!
Faute de mieux, I made a virtue of my contradictions –
humour was the one weapon to unseat the era.
But when I started hearing panic behind the mockery
the joke had come too close to home.

Tomtoms drummed me back at night from the Big Arch –
Speer's neo-geo paradigm, marmoreal in white Carrara –
to a counter-city in the galleries at Châtelet.
I took the pons asinorum to maturity,
chose a destiny, lit up, went back to my subterfuge.

Beside me, in the next block, lived the ultimate collector.
I never saw him, only heard the poisoned whisperings:
one day they called the *pompiers* in to clean him out,
houseproud among a decade's scatological relics,
each one labelled, wrapped and catalogued.

Hyperborean

Beyond the north, they got lost,
vertical man and the errant
evangelist. It was a country
gawping like their own, somehow
more so, too often, Puzzled,
they peered into the dusk
and watched a stunned light
sink across the Islands

of the Blessed. Dry skin
feathered, water turned to bone
in the saucepan left outside
beneath the fur and fog.
Stars were logged, fear and sloth;
one sermon for the monitor,
another for the fire-worshipper.
Mercury burst its tongue

in the grizzly sub-zero
of ultimate stasis, congealed
exhaust, noontime of God's
abrupt ignition. Fish-blooded,
they seeped down, inwards,
where air and cold had seeded
spruce theologies. Sleet
would drift in too, moaning

a prayer for the thrawn
puritan light of imperious
snowmen. White nights, shrill
warranties. Fulfilment
was something promise couldn't
touch, not knowing why
intent hatched out to vacancy
and ambition climbed

like an abrupt solar congress,
scorching the sleeves
of damp and distant cities,
only to stoop, lunge
and come to ground, misery's
plumage, in pack ice. Sometimes
they wept to be themselves;
embarrassed, but only to weep.

Guesses multiplied to years.
They bent in punitive cold
for an earnest of their atonement;
its dread and drama. No knock
would ever bear them out
but they guarded their cramped
station against spooks, frost,
thuggish nights. Sleeping,

they collided, appalled to find
motive had declared itself,
no inquest made, in the journey's
jargon. Another thought
trudged back to its one sure
place, the empty offices.
Farther on, the moral. Slowly
distance stopped chanting,

then they. No head could hold
what hope heaped up, extravagant
orator of the opposing view.
There was only one, in that sound.
Sea was blue-bleak, obedient
to any epilogue, all and none;
slapdash of its slow wet
in a hard cold, beyond the north.

Hotel Savoy
Homage to Joseph Roth

Call me Gabriel, bearer of bad tidings.
Today we're waiting for Bloomfield
to rescue us from ourselves, and the old world.

Some have refused morphine, others to believe.
The rest have drunk themselves drowned
and all they know is: 403 has been with 41.

On a day like this, of ironic disbelief,
more than the K & K has gone for good.
Soldiers without an eagle ride through town

to the rhythm of Frau Kupfer's girls
peddling water on the floorboards underneath.
Stasia, she's sublimating the Variétés

and Herr Fisch cooking up a lottery winner,
but to no avail: no one leaves the hotel
or its seven draughty floors, no one except

Zwonomir, weeping over his cows, swearing
on America. Sour Ignatz hopes it too...
Nothing gets done except dreaming

and the impossible business of renaming streets,
something the walls know, yellow with smoke,
witness to a hundred drafts and revisions

and fear like a trapped breath on the stairs.
The public death is a private one:
history loses its rag in a grotty corner

while a brass-band brays the imperial anthem
and laughter emptying from the bay-windows
of small hotels, Europe's many mansions

tells of ordinary things that leave us burning.
As it is, only beds endorse our bodies...
In mine I find poppyseeds, a sweet premonition.

But things more urgent that her svelte shape
are moving us westwards like a continent;
love is difficult, and beyond the baggy curtains

a city is hungry. Then we fall between two
evils: being alone, and our brief idea
of leaving, that it might be worse elsewhere.

The Society of Mystic Animals

This jackdaw's called Kafka. He speaks German. From his vantage, the molehills may well be dug-outs.

But they're not. They're listening posts for the life that happens next.

And this is it, by hook or crook.

In another sense it's not: it's a story beyond remedy. We'll get the point of it soon enough.

It opens with the passover wind. Already spring – a panic god – is coiled in the undergrowth. Farm implements hide, head down, in the topsoil.

A bobbin under the farmer's daughter's chair slowly disembowels itself.

Dogs turn alarmist, hovering above the daily lesson. If only they'd stop pitying us so much.

Stoats tap the tree-spirits for a replica of the cryptic Christ, then run amock among the impassive hooded herbivores knee-deep in marram.

Toads amass by the road, craving acceleration. They're tub-thumpers, to a toad.

A curtain of moths, observing a long cohort of weevils defiling by the garden path, has surrendered completely. Evangelists of the candle-flame.

Owls wink in unison, heretical godfathers to the moles strung upside-down as traitors. There's one for every telegraph pole from Borodino to Sarajevo.

We're all sitting ducks, and the rats have pulled the plug on us.

The joke, such as it is, is a weasel. The cowed compliant ruminants, peddling air till first light, have been trying to keep it in the family. They'll get it in the neck.

The more you know, the less you understand. Even the swine run away with our sins.

On the way out the mice sing *Weinen, Klagen, Sorgen, Zagen.* The sound slowly rends.

A bestial moment, but one that releases us. Now we know there are things we can't have, for love or money. If only our feet would carry us away. But feet, and more than feet, have been undermined.

And so it was, for some years after, that the letter K became a shamefaced mendicant, wandering without honour among its own people.

A Land –
(Gottfried Benn, 1933)

A land, a turbid sea,
then the flukes and glimmers
of an outlandish empire
like a rumour scotching its source.

Night and day, a neither-nor.
Gut fears, death like the Gadarene –
Land of the Gone-to-Ground –
it's somewhere you were born...

Silhouettes stake out claims
to the sedan-chairs and Louis Quinze;
tongue-biters, old boys
take in the scene, and hunker down.

All those whose squint through tears
at the daily annulments,
free spirits too, and Men of Light:
they're on the watch, and nearer.

Translating the Translators

I.
They called it
user-friendly –
it was the DIY
of a lethal dose.

Still, ghostwriting
its *hors-texte*
revolution made
us word-perfect,

unable to resist
those subliminal
slogans for the One
True Science

whose built-in
obsolesence
would one day cry
havoc and leave

us streetwise.
Heroes of the late
great 19th
century trampled

all over us
when we valorized
the trivium's
hoedown stomp.

II.
They called us
what they liked
in the Institute
of Unlikeliness.

We were token
Esperantists,
sidestepping Mez-
Voio, Globaqo,

Ido, Ekselsioro
(airy sons of a hare-
lipped Volapükist)
to propagate

the best-selling
maxims of universal
understanding,
the consumer's

Babel-binary.
We pulled the wraps
off God's bitter-
sweet tautologies;

then conspired
like true
professionals
against the laity.

III
The Word was
quarantined
but the germ-line's
wigwam marks

survived the century
to end them all
in a bin marked
Extraterritoriality.

We turned in its
stunned velocities
for a clumsily
vital stasis

so we could face
each other
the next morning
without having

to rehabilitate
those lumpy clichés
where a patriot
comes indoors

from the cold
to a happy ending
and a huge hug
from our Leader.

IV
One old colleague
who'd lost
his entire family
in the last war

was still engrossed
in the rawly
immaculate data
of his persecutors.

Translating pain
into an amnesty
for word-shy
nominalists

he could sometimes
hear a routine
of trapped sobs,
an undertaker

sniggering
at his comic-strip
solecisms. Once
he was frogmarched

through the barracks
to a free lunch
on our sponsor's
hot money.

V
We hauled it
back from the brink,
our Houyhnhnmic
overdraft;

declassified
the hit lists,
pulped the master
narrative.

Trouble was
the facts wouldn't
ever speak
for themselves

and we drew
a blank, talking
shop to the absent-
minded victims.

In the real
world of unemployment
there was no safe
house and truth

was a booby-
trapped removal
van idling
in the no-go zone.

VI
Two redundant
syllables –
and the proofs
went skiting out

the half-open window
into the arms
of a revisionist.
It was a point

of no return –
nobody said
who'd got the word-
count wrong.

Before the glib
original sin
of every clerk
there hadn't been

a metaphor
in standing sight.
We told them
what they asked

to hear and left,
startled how
we'd lisped a single
motherly dialect.

Terms of Reference

When you finally leave the flatlands of Trial and Error
and enter the citadel of Fatal Surprises –
one oppressed by facts, the other argued from design –
you'll notice, like me, how the sea-stain leaves your mouth,
becoming something alien in a cursory landscape
of concrete prefabs and functional grey.

Past the post-office and the sinister lampposts
you're crossing, with a tic of recognition,
the frontier of Seriousness.
On one side, compassion-dispassion is a Gemini trait;
elsewhere, like a declaration of dishonesty,
the messages home will never be harder.

It's a journey you've made so often
the mock-sinister graffiti and deflationary motifs
hardly deflect you from the task.
What it is you have to do has never been said aloud,
but you'll work through it painstakingly
till it bites down to the quick.

Choice hardly comes into it now.
Already, in the open air, phrases are dilating.
Inside thin walls, behind stale curtains,
a body has shrunk into itself.
Soon it'll be part of the decor,
running, if only it knew how, down the dim corridors.

Deadpan bearer of the caduceus, Job's comforter,
remember how far it is to the horizon –
the old ones aren't shamming
and the last metaphor they'll accomodate
runs dribbling down their chins.
Past caring, they'll stop keeping up appearances.

In the glossaries of fear and excrement
souls are less reclaimable than the rights of man –
loose enjambments, ruptures, a small theatre
where consciousness drills the audience
for luminous departures, clearings of the day.
No protocol, but those are your terms of reference.

One interpretation says: the man without proof is an enemy.
Another: life goes on by different means
but only in parable, on a day of public unconcern,
when spouses scatter the tell-tale signs
at night, between countries,
and what was most itself fits the unspecial dark.

Turn back to where you broke the day like an egg.
None of this is authorized
and when you return through the daytime zodiac
to bodies which forget their lines
what you'll see is this professional landscape.
Words – neutral, companionable – begin to drown again.

Snake and Horse
Two shamanistic scat-songs

1. Snake

I know you. You don't know me.
My name is Snake. Just call me Doc.
I'm blowing you clean. I'm sounding out the bad.
This is your sickness. Its smell is strong.
My name is Snake. Just call me Doc.
I've starved your wife to get it right.
Ten days of grubs and ants. Mean Moses stuff.
My name is Snake. Just call me Doc.
No scrub suit man. No ice. No stainless steel.
You're sick. I don't talk guff. I don't talk sham.
Bright good can't say its thin white name.
Just listen in. This is the wrong. Snug in your skin.
My name is Doc. The harm is out. Go with the sun.
You find your life. You lose it next.

2. Bring Your Horse

When the sickness comes, bring it to the sweathouse.
Bring your red horse, tobacco and beer gut too.
We'll talk till the sickness is cross-eyed
and the sun is gone, swinging through the dark.
I won't make you shit snakes or piss in the wind
but you'll say the names and won't look away:
Sorrow Running Wild, Flogged Horse, Old Dog in Heat.
Your sickness is climbing out of the world
and it won't be today, my Passamaquoddy friend,
hammocks or backbones yield to the maker of mountains.

Mile Zero

After the Azores
came lazy spouts of brine
and the herring reek
of Cape Breton where Gaelic
was a suggestive drift

in the blather and gab-gash;
wet-proofed, shipped
across water like a New Deal
or modernity's degree
zero. Even the recalcitrant

trade-winds mated with a seal
form of the goddess
Nuliajuk (whose soapstone
replica holds house
from my blustery desk),

as if X marked the spot
where history turned itself
in, becoming geography,
and the punctilious
cartographers of the margin

had to go incognito, shod
with nothing more
than kinship's clandestine
onus, the Celtic
left-brain turning tables

on itself while a westerly
yammered like Moses
with a maxim, cotton waft
from the Carolinas
scouting up the Irish Sea

to tend a palm tree
on the harsh brackish
shore of the mother-country.
Farther south, the first
and last Scottish colony

was a banana republic
where the Chief of the Rains
speared himself praying
to the motmot birds
and someone punned in Navajo

that the new world
was as old as the hills;
unaccustomed to rum
and self-pity in Key West
and the Gulfstream

easing by with news
from Cartagena's mosquito
coast to the Windwards,
it must have seemed
a Sargasso of daydreams –

rescheduling the work-ethic
to watch a leaf storm
set up shanties
in the Hesperides...
Despite our near-legendary

frugality, someone else
was about to spring
potlatch and make us chew
the Germanic root
for giving gifts, daft

days in the drab
backstreets of a northern city
with its Boston grid
and arsenal of endearments
where pen-pushers rise

from their sedentary life
to squint over the horizon,
remembering from tobacco
days that going west
was Jacobethan for a wake

reversed.

The Burden of the Past

One half of the city can be discounted
like a macadam mirage or a klaxon on high C,

or trundled out among the desert
hosannahs of fire escapes and pharmacies.

Tiny zinc roofs shiver in the haze
and a roller-coaster lies spellbound on its side

like the symbol for infinity. The city's seal
is a fossil fish sweltering in amber

for the crutch Christ. Today, only the dead
know what it means, and why the clergy,

disappearing down the sewers, spit
furtively at the billboards. Each ample day

brings another narrative of misdirections,
odd headlines, pollen, magpie summers

when a city floats like a kite – hats off,
hats flying, hats huddled up and trampled on.

If you should need one for the bright
clear nights (when it's cold enough to cure TB)

then try the lost property offices
conveniently situated on major thoroughfares.

★

In the clockmakers' ghetto, you might run
across the other half, or find it

subversively depicted on an Easter egg.
On its dusty corners, in a swim of shoppers,

bronze pioneers stand together for warmth
or company, conspicuously unnoticed

wrestlers who've spent the last twenty years
proclaiming providence to a parking lot.

Today, and only today, you'll grasp
the principle: cities are founded on loss.

Knowing it too, but sneezing hopefully,
people come out of doors to hide

in public, reading weather from the view
of minor Alps and wind-dazzled spaces.

Traffic bleats behind you. Soon a speculative
downpour will rest on your conscience.

You traverse the south with its steep
broad day, its realignments of the given,

as desert lisps beyond the choke-weeds
where settlement began, slowly becoming formal.

IV

Bags and Iron

The sun burst through
at a muzzy executioner's hour
on torn tin roofs
and weatherboard houses perched
along the dust-bowl
plateau where the Barrier Range

took issue with Bromide Street.
The whitewashed hospital
groaned like an empire steamship
that had forced the pace
from Colonel Light's model city
and the end-littoral

of the ballast continent
seized as bounty
because reason was singing glory
in his London house...
Cumulus slid on greased rails
over my bush-citadel,

pariah town of one-word miners,
sad wives maddened
by distance and loneliness;
somewhere I'd come
to avoid poems, to get
lost in work and an ocean

of sheer descant,
those boiling diorama sunsets
on the Mundi Mundi plains.
Beyond the Great Divide
tar dribbled out in turmeric,
a single epithet of scrub

proclaimed bush Quarantina –
the dormant life
of monoliths and plebiscites,
mass graves for sheep
that couldn't sell, the ultimate
closed shop. I held out

for a year, Stakhanovite
on suffrance, mending the icons
like Bukgakov in his Notebook.
I read the law, its black and white,
and what green ants revised.
When the radio voices

sank, and the fly-choir barbecues,
I went underground
through all the metaphors of depth –
solomonic, confessional –
down in up out through seams
of safety and risk

to the bigger town beneath –
an inorganic, artesian journey...
At night I slid across
its black hydraulic surfaces,
immured, engulfed
in the weight of silence,

like a booby-trap left behind
by Captain Nemo. I had
less time than that to disabuse
myself when the sun
torched screeds of banksias
and the galahs shrieked

over florid eggs
and hugely incandescent distances.
It walked me home across
business and salt
and the egotistical sublime
laid out in strata

at my feet, bags and iron
and the rare earths
of Australia's eco-blues
caught in a crust
of self-contempt. In the red
centre of embarrassing

faces and heavy industry
nobody ever talked of progress.
After a year of broken
English, bliss was as much
as anyone could hope for, verst on verst
running like an elevator

through daytime sleep
to the single disaffectionate
thought of every convict:
if I headed north
I'd probably find myself
walking backwards to China.

Polynesia

Between Pitcairn and Norfolk
is about as other as you'll ever get,

a harbour bottom exposed to oils
and opulence and the silted

channel where a phthisic Scot
stepped out at the world's end,

not in the Name of God but
holding instructions for fury.

★

Afternoon collapses on the hills.
The last tuna goes on ice

and corned beef cans come floating in
over banked shoals of cliché.

'The word is out, and the doom
written,' wrote Mr Stevenson,

expelling smoke through the view
that sucked in German Apia.

★

Nowadays the only flotillas
are parasols. Beside the halogen

cross of the Mormon Tabernacle
a dog creeps into the pen.

What litters the bright jetties
next morning is trade's high-flown

rhetoric, straggly convocations
of irascible neighbours.

★

On Sundays, pigs let off steam
and choirs hurl hymns across the bay.

If you're dreaming of Gaugain's
uncertain children running the waves

to meet you, a parallel clan
of keelhaulers and beachcombers,

then look behind... Captain can't
stand the sea: *la foule*, resurgent.

★

The thistle is used to bereavement,
injustice, the smell of burning.

No window encloses it. The hibiscus
presses on the page, a sweet

imbibition. It outrages dark
familiar Bible-lands, the covenant

just coming to, rebuffed by gratitude
on the Road of the Loving Hearts.

Living in a Dry Place

This is it at last,
Hesiod's update
on the Work and Days.
Look for a hotel.
Ask for directions even.
He's not listening –
grinding his own axe
and nobody else
beside him, trepanning
the creaky verandah
as a wedge-tail
lifts, hanging out over
space and stillness.
The rest is literature.
After the cool
experiment, read this
back-of-Bourke
manifesto from the land
of Oz, dromedary
sleep and bush meanings –
a gnawed-at muster
the dogs dig up –
and think of hiding
under the tropics.
You can't stare it out.
So throw it back,
and look what's
coiling round your boots:
a glottal shrug
so far gone in history
it sucks stones.

Month of knowing when we get there

*

Month of keeping the wind on a string

*

Month of the hesitant heat

*

Month of red rime on the verandah

*

Month of city streets on air

*

Month of the kangaroo hecatomb

*

Month of the long outdoors and no house by the sea

*

Month of spitting the grape-cluster stars

*

Month of the custodial deaths

*

Month of galahs on the generators

*

Month of looking back to see what's coming

*

Month of ending in embraces

Lake Deception, Mount Fortitude;
the bottler names labour in translation

like an apocryphal oral version
of the Book of Revelation, a page from Bunyan

that would combust proof and patent
if you ever held them up

to the weatherbeaten millions.
The wind has forgotten its last sentence,

ruffling the ice-crack pleasantries
of the desert solitary standing on the porch

to welcome you, odd visionary tourist
with your anti-Baedeker, beef jerky and shortwave.

You've come to see an original affluent society
outstare its own beginnings.

Nobody's digging for yams, though.
That stuff went out with coal republics,

farmers who loathed the Age of Reasonableness
and trains that ran on separate gauge...

Now the slogans read: give up grog
and the Lucky Country will rescue you from history,

airlifting a metaphor to anyone lost for one
beyond the quondong trees and billabongs.

Finally they reach an understanding
with the stringybarks, the shamefaced bush.
What's left folds away its placenta
for a rainy day with scribs of spinifex.
Off-camera, a nation turns its back
on the interior, the dry place where sand
makes monkey business of the maps
and explorers think they've hit Shit Creek.
They put it in a box and walk away,
and what's left is screened from sight:
blunt men doing their business underground
in the lodes of silence between cities.

Out in the barrens
you allow yourself one dangerous thought:
You, Great Heart, are the enemy.

Language glares at the landscape
but you dig down deeper,
shirt belling between shoulderblades,

till the adjectives tumble across dry
paddocks and salt-pans,
warp and vector of the marvellous.

Then heat stands up like a preacher
under the eye of heaven,
airy, face to face, gone from under.

Gazeteer of the Bush, you'd smother the idea –
a year as broken-backed as a holiday.
No author ever died here, among the artisanal

ploughshares and sunflower Fibonaccis
but the book-shy do, and their names are uplift.
What's gravity, you ask the red river gums

at the savannah's edge, red-brown inclines
that wear out strides and loneliness.
A giant levity rings off ancient casuarinas

standing on shoulders, in earshot of the surf.
Your father's dogged stomp. We wade down
to the Wang Wauk, through purple hills and valleys

and the domesday names of Mr Spectator's Ukania:
only Boeotians, you quip, know the cure
for zimzim words and Geneva's milky doctrine,

the translatorese of Standard Average European.
Head-down in the dark, inverted bulwarks
prop up the albatross cities. Cedars of Lebanon.

We sit outside, among kumquats and persimmons,
exulting in the ordinary. What happens
is something put back, pondered, sprung from.

You drive into this space.
Its meaning is where you stop between
hard work and idleness,
and people who've read their minds.

They cross to the bare heart of things,
street names, oxidised ambition:
Krypton, Iodide, Sulphide, Argent.
A rebuke of turps and camphor.

You watch a racking cloud-cargo
assemble from the Roaring Forties
and dip precipitously over Antarctica.
Habitat becomes enchantment.

Then you drive out of this space
and prepare yourself to say:
he's gone, she's turned her back.
You trip on the words. One long last look.

Is this the place, I asked the farmer,
where the first people painted the ceiling?
Wouldn't have the blindest, mate,
I just lip the wind here.
This ain't no bleedin' Nag Hammadi.
Soon enough, I limped from the light.

It was like wanting to curse God
only to be told by the Turin Evangelist
that he'd died, in 1882.
The year, incidentally, this town
consisted of ten tin shacks, a corner pub
and a single open-cast.

Mined-out a century later
some of my patients were still dreaming
of tenements and sewing machines,
Prague, pigeons, twilights, flu.
Others lapsed into Serbo-Croat at the first sign.
So where were we, in fathoms or fetters?

Mother-wit, I suppose, kept them going;
silver, zinc, lead, and hatred of uniforms;
free outdoor swimming lessons
and the heroic days, before fridge-freezers.
The young still left in droves,
driving miles and miles to smell the sea.

I wasn't going to make them virtuous,
but I called on some
before the afternoons went toxic.
Remember, said one old miner
who'd lived through drought; in this life
happy folk are past praying for.

O come into your desolation
Sing a trekker's song of destination

You're a pioneer of the one true nation
Come serve it with a convocation

Disarm it with its destitution
The citizen's rights in the constitution

Bore it stiff with trite conversation
The thready story of your true conversion

But don't forget the mission
The settler's song of free admission

So come into your desolation
Come tourist it with deconstruction

And you'll be this, an inadmissible admission
(What the manual calls an odd misprision)

After the totem grog, nothing goes without saying
except the three ways out: *t'Adelaide*, *upriver*
and *gone bush*. The last is pure allure
like a bare thoughtfulness of trees on the Darling,
beating about the uplands, lightning underground.

*

Never rained on, memory stands on the porch
and peers across a poky backyard at a used car lot,
the torpid peace of a hard metallic town.
Terror is everywhere, like a gap in the traffic,
afraid of nothing except the neighbours.

*

A city creeps back to itself, to serious drink
and the bush unzipping its nasty surprises,
dry gulchs called Last Ditch. Zinc ablatives
and bloody cursing wonders rise above
corrugated shouts, slagheaps, straining faces.

*

There's no name yet for the watertank's ironic chant
or the spiky unassailability of a mythic geography,
faces ablaze as the desert drives into town
like an anthropologist with a grudge against travellers.
One thing, mate: leave, and you've failed the test.

Anthropology of an Island
for Neil Risk

No easy access like Trobriand
and not a place of refuge for old dictators

doing a crash-course on Suetonius. Less inbred
than Tristan da Cunha, nearly innocent

of the wine-dark. One rainmaker
per ten thousand inhabitants, no binding

contract for results. A littoral
studded with long-faced meridional artefacts

holding their breath while Kontiki
breaks up on the surf. More creationist

than Galapagos, surreal as Celebes; its tourists
parted by keels, rescued by the trade-gap

and another rendezvous with summer.
Required reading for potential

immigrants: *Leviathan.* Viking settlements
in the main street and a flagpole

magnetized due north. A floating capital
carted off the weather-map even

in the roaring days of oil-boom investments.
It deposits itself around you

with its fish-smells and rumours
of self-sufficiency, peradams in the basalt.

Clambers down behind you at the edge
of a Faroese summer, to collect the bottles.

The Real Thing

It turned, I guess, on what a man was.
That, and the wives adjudicating in the pastures,
keen as sorrow and the slack agape
of a doughty land, oaths spat out like limes.
  If words are deeds, said the Brothers,
  the pilgrim rest is guess. They'd
  read the Book, but what it said
  was something else again.

They slammed life shut, or left it like a box
intact. Under the sky no piercing wonder
measured to the mission, a country of the empty coat.
Time made them weep, snake-bruising men.
  The greatest sin, another said,
  is standing still. So they
  chased the wind, but where it led
  was somewhere else again.

Mountains walked ahead, and the heart wasn't humble.
No doors opened; company became an eerie
stock indifference. Wind rearranged the plains
and made them sleep aslant, in attitudes to marvel at;
  only thinking, never asking why
  the work got done. Whoever
  knew was keeping quiet
  about the Altogether Else.

At the Mission Hall, you could hear the hush.
Out of the whale's guts, across quilted pastures,
engines coughed at an old adversity
of quags and basalt. Scapegraces shifted feet
  groping in the dark
  for the breathing last who'd gone
  before. What they smelled
  was something altogether else.

So it came, the whispering hearsays, the unkindnesses.
In the slopping tanks, water was a rude resource.
Heifers told all there was of solidarity;
so long husbanded to the land only they could say
    there was no other boast,
    choosing silence and entering
    it, a catalogue of know-how
    and almost nothing else.

And after all, at the leathery sea, here at last
was land that hurt like home, flintlock folk
all singing the song instead of this.
Hope sprouted, thrived where nothing else would grow,
    a thistle emblematic of itself,
    God's unkempt family being the first
    to milk the antidote, one fine
    day, all else having failed.

Sons and Pioneers

After retinal close-down
the usual white noise.
We sat about, fidgeting,
till one of us stumbled
across his voice again
and the boy's-own spoor
of the missing link
slid around the fire,
cowering from our torches.
Our scapegoat was pegged
down for the night
to appease the weather,
the old story thudding
its tomtom in our blood
like the exact science
of a one-man band;
but before we plotted
our course from A to B
across the airy savannahs
of our lost estate,
we read back by marsh-light
to the illegible graffiti
obscuring the subways,
and calmly appropriated
the undefended future:
an ominous pall of defeat
settled like coal-dust
on the tatty regalia
of last year's winners –
sons of the corporation,
pioneers of the field-trip.
By the mercury sumps
we auctioned the jeeps,
and felt the loose change
of half a lifetime

burning like worry-beads
in our sweaty palms...
When morning came
swooping down the glades
we picked ourselves up
where we'd left off,
surplus to the sum
of our own requirements.
No baggage, no ideas;
just tinnily resonant
myths of the good life
that led no farther
than the garden gate
and those drab precursors
who wouldn't take.
They clung to us
like terrified children
who couldn't say
what the message was
(it looked like a trick
to bleed us dry
with crocodile tears);
hanging around downwind
in twos and threes
where a leased-out hoarding
proclaimed the latest saga
of public grievances
and private come-uppances:
the mud redemption
of yesterday's hard men.
But the past got worked up
as we went along –
imperfect, conditional,
nothing to hold against
the sad vibrating
sympathy of quartz,
though it might have been
something we confused

with the damp verdicts
of a small country
on that day the clouds
lifted like diplomats
and the onlookers – shy
at the need for words –
remembered what it
meant, the moody climate
sobbing down gutters,
corridors where voices go,
bus-stands, bleery
dazzlements of neighbours.
We watched a street
baffle the serious wind,
factories enter judgement
under the neon wink
of new money, entrances
and exits and dutiful
say-no-more updates
on who did what to whom
the very night before.
We had grounds for hope,
figuring in several,
though the version we heard
was bronchial, a human
haar around the making-do
of queues and slack time;
janitorial afterlives
whose meaning escaped us
even as we knocked.
In the locust calendar
where sons leave home
and return as fathers,
we were never far away
from the old voices.
Then it began to rain:
they had other things to do
and went indoors.

Words of One Syllable

Who knows why they leave, but they do.
The wind flaps, and gives no sign
though the risk breathes a hint of wolf.
They boast, they limp out on a curse
though they can't tell which. Sheep look up
coal-faced, at the edge of the deep.

They yawn, they nod, they look and loom,
and love, it goes to a dark shed.
This is the word, and this is the life
spat on, got through, worn out, gone from.
Old hats are damp where heads are:
deep in the ground, dense in the air.

Dark folds of days would mean as much.
Small fish get worked to the bone.
And down the mines, the air is sour;
grown cold, it creeps in the door
to tea and scones. They feed on that,
sit side by side, and talk true grit.

Who knows, the days could mean no worse.
The harm is done and sons go out
though they walk on salt and dig for less.
Faces at the door are all at sea
when one says, dear, it'll be fine but.
Now they leave not a word says not.

Works

One way or other, we all come to this drab outhouse, its plainest sense of things. Pretending you're an engineer or aviator is, let's be kind, a *déformation professionelle.*

In the pastoral hour life surrenders for a song. What bows out is a moral or a marriage.

They won't come, they'll just send their bodies. Tell them these are the symbols. The symbols say that they must die. Or: they say that they must change their life, and still meet the cost.

Be literal: life's always lurking somewhere in the sentence.

Comfort can be measured by how many hearts have drowned in a cup of tea. Pity gets about on rollers, pushed by the porters. Laughter leaves its lungs behind.

What you're hearing is an either / or, a question of logic and lesions. Neither is very deep. Learn to curse, and that oxygen is a voodoo word of great power and purity. Ask, but don't expect answers.

Pain forgets what it means. Fear runs on the spot, very fast. Inside the skin are onion bandages and the root cause. Something has worn itself out. It replaces itself with words. But that's an alien concept: already you've stepped back in disgust, from the wallpaper, or this idea of man.

Up to a point, care and cure are the same word. Most people get better without help. This is a demonstration.

Beware the stories. Some are in dialect, coming out of slander and slaughter and elaborate long insults. The dead, who'd give anything to have their say, manage a kind of white noise, miles below the surface.

Remember these are mortal accents, by-blows. One day, when you least expect it, they'll humble you of bright excuses.

Distrust imagination: it's always ready, a cool professional, to cork the orifices.

If it's an epic, it's one of endurance and enormous effort. There's always another dimension beyond diagnosis, another soft book. This one's in a rage for the real. If it woke there, it'd be shocked by its heartlessness.

More than ever you can't renounce, which, in a word, means nothing's exempt.

Learn the argument against yourself. Here's a message from home: *send word, between here and midnight.*

Rain Diary

You hardly have to say the word and it's here, hauling
Banff Bailiffs across the streets of Europe
to one of Joyce's reclaimed 'funams of waste arenary soil',
Nora breathing 'O Jim!' the very day he stopped
in the Bleibtreustrasse and watched it pour down flights,
his nation's *esprit de l'escalier*. Reading it
is like explaining a heresy, its one-offs and torrents
soodling, dropwise, sklent notations of delight.
It takes women of the sun cultures indoors, fingers
in every recess. Damp clothes drop like names
in the rue de la Cherche-Midi, soft exclamations
and no talk of respite, only poor men and pike staves.
Half an hour later, like Mercutio, it recalls them
to the ordinary. Beyond the comic the credible;
but that was before it had gone a while down-under
and swept a town off its feet. It disappears inside itself
like an enharmonic pun; its iron cataracts yielding
a blue moon to the platitudes of assent
blowing upwards sheer off mountains. Vigil levels out
in its aftermath. It mists futures, pocks stone
with slow acids, leaving no one outside
dragging neighbours to his wake while the moon
slumps in the midden. Some keep it in clay pots, hoping
a flaff will dry it on the change or temper
the peaty spirit, its sublimation of the very worst.
Like Vico's history, it's a spatial form of coming back;
rigorously errant, faithful to its origins.
Hospitality grows from watersigns, its toponymic limbo.
Undemonstrative, it dumps chill messages,
finds lovers everywhere, scuffing down from saga-steads
like serendipity, striking out the excursus
it once made to an attentive rapt face on the watergaw
fixed half a childhood over the Broomielaw. Our pluvial towns
step out of history, and watch themselves get wet.